KNITTING

A Beginner's Guide

Jeannine
Romer

Knitting: A Beginner's Guide is also available in accessible formats for people with any degree of visual impairment. The large print edition and e-book (with accessibility features enabled) are available from Need2Know. Please let us know if there are any special features you require and we will do our best to accommodate your needs.

First published in Great Britain in 2013 by
Need2Know
Remus House
Coltsfoot Drive
Peterborough
PE2 9BF
Telephone 01733 898103
Fax 01733 313524
www.need2knowbooks.co.uk

Contents

Introduction

Why knit?

Learning to knit can be a fun and rewarding experience. There are many benefits to learning to knit for yourself and others. Knitting is an enjoyable pastime you can use to create beautiful items for yourself, your home and for others. You can learn to knit to express your own style and to add useful items to your wardrobe that you couldn't buy in a shop. You can create gifts for others that show how much you care; and, at the same time, you will be spending less money than it would cost to purchase ready-made. But, you may be asking yourself, can I learn to knit?

Anyone can learn to knit. It is a skill that men, women, children, the elderly, people who are home-bound, busy professionals and stay-at-home parents can use.

Does knitting have any benefits?

Knitting has been shown to help one's health as well. It is a great way to relax after a stressful day. Knitting is also used as a therapy for those suffering from depression, anxiety, post-trauma stress, and conditions such as attention deficit hyperactivity disorder. It is being used in prisons to teach anger management, goal-orientation, focus and patience. The repetitive nature of knitting is good for your immune system too. It causes changes in brain chemistry that lower blood pressure, heart rate and stress hormones; while at the same time, it increases the brain's feel-good chemicals, serotonin and dopamine. Knitting is relaxation for your mind and body, comparable to meditation, and you have something you can be proud of for your finished product.

How long will it take?

How long it takes to learn to knit is up to the individual. Each person is different. We each learned to walk, talk and ride a bicycle at our own pace. So, have patience with yourself as you learn. You will be teaching your hands to do something new, and it takes a while to build up the muscle memory in your hands as they practise this new skill. If you become frustrated at any point, stop and take a break. This is good practice for many skills including knitting. But, don't give up! Even skilled knitters need to practise new techniques until they 'get it right' or read a pattern over and over again until they understand how it works. You will feel a sense of accomplishment and a boost of self-esteem as you develop in the art and skill of knitting.

Celebrities knit too!

When you learn to knit you will be in great company. Many famous people have been knitters, and many film actors have taken up knitting as an easy-to-put-down time filler while waiting between scenes. Actors such as Russell Crowe, David Arquette, Debra Messing and Tim Daly have taken up knitting. Scarlett Johansson has a pattern in *Fabulous Designs at Hollywood's Knitting Circle*, by Edith Eig.

Tracy Ullman has co-authored a book *Knit 2 Together* with Mel Clark, who owns a knitting shop in Los Angeles.

Have patience with yourself

Anyone can learn to knit. Use this pastime to create wonderful items for your wardrobe, beautiful gifts for family and friends, and gain health benefits associated with the craft. Learning to knit can make you happier and healthier. You can knit to donate to many charities and know that your knitting is good for others too. It will also allow you to make fine quality items at a fraction of the cost in a shop. Have patience with yourself and in no time you will be knitting and feeling great.

Chapter One
Knitting Equipment and Accessories

How do I choose needles?

Selecting knitting needles and yarn can be a daunting task to the beginner. Knitting needles come in a wide range of sizes and materials. The important thing to remember is that you choose what feels good to your fingers. The needle size will depend upon the yarn that you choose. Knitting needles are made from aluminium, wood, bamboo and plastic. Each material has a different feel to your hands and a different approach to the yarn. Aluminium and plastic needles allow the yarn to slip easily on the needle. Wood and bamboo needles have a measure of stickiness and do not allow for ease of slip. They are internationally standardised in sizes from 14 to 000 (2mm to 17mm).

Needle Size Conversion Chart

Metric	Imperial	US
2mm	14	0
2.25mm	13	1
2.5mm	12	**
2.75mm	12	2
3mm	11	3
3.25mm	10	3
3.5mm	9	4
3.75mm	9	5
4mm	8	6
4.5mm	7	7
5mm	6	8
5.5mm	5	9
6mm	4	10
6.5mm	3	10.5
7mm	2	**
7.5mm	1	**
8mm	0	11
9mm	00	13
10mm	000	15

This chart shows the sizes of knitting needles in imperial, metric and US sizes. I am including this chart so that if you have family heirloom needles, or car boot sale finds, you will be able to tell a little more about your needles. However, the metric measurements are the most commonly used.

The basic needles are straight, come in a pair, and are used to knit flat pieces. Double pointed needles come in packages of four or six. They are used to knit a seamless tube (knitting in the round) for hats, mittens, gloves and jumpers. Circular knitting needles have two points connected by a plastic wire, also for knitting in the round, or for very wide shawls. There are also cable needles that are used for holding stitches that are going to be crossed in cable patterns. Other supplies you will need are a needle gauge, which can also be used to measure your gauge.

'A needle gauge is a great tool.'

You will also need a ruler (a clear one allows you to see your stitches through the ruler); a tape measure for those larger projects that need measuring; a yarn needle with a large eye for any sewing up you need to do at the end; and a small pair of scissors that will fit in your knitting kit. You may also like to purchase a knitting bag to carry your project with you wherever you go. My daughter-in-law made one for me. It has lots of pockets inside and out and plenty of room inside for an entire jumper project.

How to select yarn

Yarns, like needles, come in different weights, materials and colours. Choosing the best quality yarn for your project will ensure that you are happy with it for years. After all, you put in the time and effort to create something wonderful, so be sure you are happy with the material used to make it.

Yarn weights in general are: lace, fingering, sport, DK, worsted and bulky. The type of project you choose determines the weight of yarn you need.

What is yarn made of?

'A project bag is a help too.'

The fibre content of yarn ranges from 100% acrylic, cotton, wool, silk and alpaca. Many yarns are blends of the aforementioned fibres with each other in varying amounts, and with other fibres such as cashmere, mohair, angora, nylon and bamboo. Cashmerino yarn from Debbie Bliss (www. debbieblissonline.com), for example, is a blend of wool, cashmere and nylon. Cotton and acrylic yarns tend to be the least expensive, while hand dyed silk, wool and alpaca tend to be the most costly. However, there are many shops that have regular sales, as well as discount shops online that have incredible sales especially of discontinued colours. Many knitters have a 'yarn stash' composed of leftover yarns and more importantly, yarn that was deeply discounted and irresistible in the shop. Yarn stashes provide instant gratification for knitting accessories, like hats, mittens and scarves. One, two and three ply yarns are used for delicate lace, baby socks and gloves. Four ply yarn is for more substantial baby clothes, heavier socks, and for lightweight tops. DK, or double knit, is suitable for most garments; it is the most widely used yarn weight. Aran weight yarn is for outdoor clothing as it has popularised the fisherman's jumper. Chunky weight is for heavier winter jumpers. Super chunky is great for beginners since it knits up quickly. It is great for scarves, coats, cushions and coverlets.

Wool/Yarn	Needle Size (approx. mm)	Uses
One, Two and Three Ply	2-3.5 mm	Delicate lace, baby socks and gloves
Four Ply	3-4 mm	Baby clothes, socks, lightweight tops
DK (Double Knit)	3.5-4.5 mm	Most knitted garments
Aran	4-5.5 mm	Outdoor clothing
Chunky	5.5-7 mm	Heavy jumpers
Super Chunky	7-12mm	Scarves, coats, hats, cushions

Where can I buy yarn?

For beginning knitters, I suggest a visit to a local yarn shop or two. There you can look at, and get a feel for, the different types of yarn and also get to know the owner or manager. Many knitting shops have a resident expert and/or classes or a knitting group that meets on a regular basis. If you are far away from a shop, or home-bound, you can order from any shop by phone or online. Please see the help list for details of online retailers in the UK.
http://planetpurl.com/planetpurl/static/showpage.htm?showpage=directory_England

The link above is a directory of yarn shops in England. The site includes an interactive list of sixty-three counties. You click on the one you live in and a list of cities and towns is generated; once you click on your home city or town a list of shops with their address and phone number appears. Your telephone directory will also provide a list of yarn shops in your area. Also, you may enquire at your local library for a knitting group that may meet there; or start one yourself! *The Friday Night Knitting Club* by Kate Jacobs is a wonderful story about just such an informal knitting group that you can find, or start, in your area.

'Yarn stashes provide instant gratification for knitting accessories, like hats, mittens and scarves.'

Summing Up

Choosing needles and yarn is a game of try it and see. It is always best to select what feels best to you. Choose the best quality of yarn at the best price for you so that you will remain happy with your creation for many years. Have patience with yourself as you learn to knit. Just like any new skill, it takes perseverance and practice. Remember, even skilled knitters learn new stitches and techniques with patience and practice.

Chapter Two

Getting Started

How to form a slip knot

Now that you have chosen your yarn and needles to begin your knitting adventure, you will learn by knitting squares in several stitches. You will use these squares to learn about gauge later in this chapter. You begin by forming a slip knot. Follow the steps below:

1. Take four or five inches of the end of the yarn in your hands.

2. Cross the loose end over the long end clockwise and hold the crossed threads between your left thumb and forefinger.

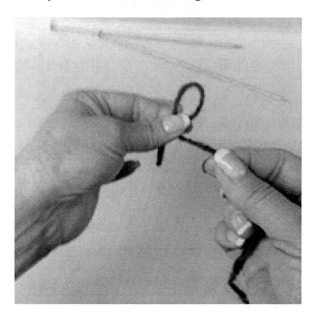

3. Take hold of the long end of the yarn between your right thumb and forefinger and push it through your first loop.

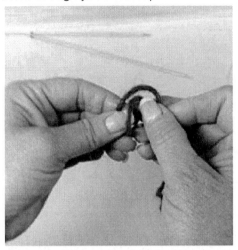

4. Tighten the knot slightly by pulling gently on the short end of the yarn

5. Place the loop of your slip knot over one needle and tighten to fit your needle, but do not pull it too tightly.

Casting on stitches

Now you are ready to begin casting on stitches. There are several methods for casting on. However, the method that follows is the simplest technique for the beginning knitter.

1. Hold the needle with the slip knot on it in your left hand, and the empty needle in your right hand.

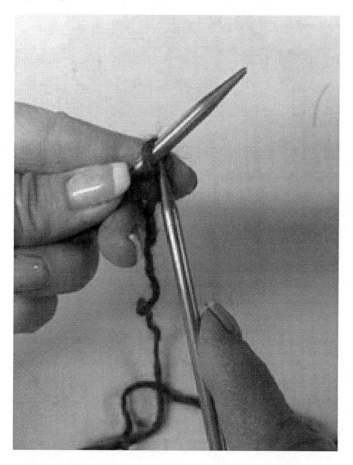

2. Push the end of the right-hand needle into the slip knot from front to back.

3. Wrap the long end of the yarn around the right-hand needle, back to front and anticlockwise so that the yarn passes between the two needles.

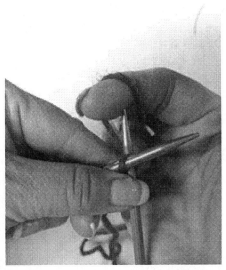

4. Using your right-hand and needle, draw the yarn through the loop on the left-hand needle. Bring it up, and twist this loop, to the top of the left-hand needle and place it over the tip and onto the left-hand needle.

5. Repeat this process until you have as many stitches (loops) on your left-hand needle as required. A good first square is to begin with twenty stitches.

The knit stitch

The garter stitch can be created by using all knit or all purl stitches (see page 20). Garter stitch is used for borders and for accents in larger pieces. We will begin with knit stitches. These are abbreviated in knitting patterns as 'k' and a number. So, for your first square you will k20. Follow the steps below:

1. Hold the needle with your stitches so it is in your left hand and the empty needle in your right.

2. Push the end of the right needle into your first stitch, from front to back. Wrap the long end of the yarn around the right-hand needle, back to front and anticlockwise so that the yarn passes between the two needles.

3. Using your right hand and needle, draw the yarn through the loop on the left-hand needle. Slip the original stitch over the end of the left needle, leaving the new loop on the right-hand needle.

4. Follow steps 1 to 3 until you have knitted all twenty stitches.

5. Row two begins by switching the full needle from your right hand to your left and beginning the process again. In patterns, this is often referred to as 'Turn and . . . '

6. You may count your stitches as you go to make sure you are keeping your stitches straight.

Troubleshooting:

■ If you have more than twenty stitches, you have forgotten to discard the worked stitch from the left-hand needle.

■ If you have a hole and less than twenty stitches, you have dropped a stitch without working it first.

■ If you have a hole and more than twenty stitches, you have wrapped the yarn over your right-hand needle twice, or wrapped the yarn over in-between stitches without working an existing stitch. This is actually an intentional technique you will learn about in chapter 8.

■ Stitches are so tight that it is difficult to knit. Relax! Your tension is showing in your knitting. Sore muscles and tight fingers show that you need to relax, take a few deep breaths and loosen up. Remember, knitting should be enjoyable and relaxing.

■ Stitches are uneven. The more you practise, the more consistent your stitches will be.

■ Stitches are too loose? Probably not; but we will discuss this later in this chapter when learning about gauge.

The purl stitch

The purl stitch is abbreviated in patterns as 'p' and a number. You can continue and complete your first square. Then switch to all purl stitches to complete your second square. Many people discover that their tension is slightly different between knit and purl stitches, don't worry; this is a learning adventure!

To purl, follow the steps below:

1. Hold your needle with the cast on stitches in your left hand and your empty needle in your right hand as before. Keep the yarn in front of your needles as you begin.

2. Push the tip of the right-hand needle into the front of the first stitch on the left-hand needle so that the right-hand needle is on top of the left.

3. Wrap the yarn clockwise around the right-hand needle.

4. Slide the tip of the right-hand needle around the left so it is now in back of the left-hand needle. You've just created a new stitch on the right-hand needle.

Need2Know

5. Slip the original stitch you just worked over the end of the left-hand needle, leaving the new loop on the right-hand needle.

6. Repeat steps 2 to 5 across your twenty stitches.

7. Row two begins by switching the full needle from your right hand to your left and beginning the process again.

How to bind off

Binding off, also known as casting off, is how one ends a piece of knitting. In general, one binds off knit stitches by knitting, and purl stitches by purling. Follow the steps below for binding off knit or purl stitches. The photos show purling off stitches.

1. Knit the first two stitches of your row.

'Binding off, also known as casting off, is how one ends a piece of knitting.'

2. Next, use the tip of the left-hand needle to pick up the first stitch knit (or purled) and lift it over the second stitch and over the end of the right needle, towards the back, discarding it in the process.

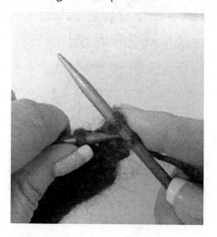

3. Knit (or purl) the next stitch on the left-hand needle. You should once again have two stitches on the right-hand needle.

4. Once again, pick up and lift the first stitch on the right-hand needle, pass it over and off.

5. Repeat steps 3 and 4 until you have just one stitch left on the right-hand needle.

6. Cut the yarn leaving a three-inch tail.

7. Pass the tail through the last stitch (loop) and pull gently to secure.

Note: Some patterns may require you to leave a much longer tail for stitching pieces together at the end.

Putting knit and purl stitches together

Most jumper patterns are knit from the bottom up. Nearly all begin with either knit one, purl one ribbing which is abbreviated in the pattern as 'k1 p1 rib'. Some jumpers, especially those knit in two or more colours, begin with knit two, purl two ribbing (k2 p2 rib) and switch colours between knit and purl stitches. This will be discussed in chapter 7.

Knit two purl two ribbing

Knit one purl one ribbing

Stockinet stitch

Stockinet stitch is less bulky than either garter stitch or knit one purl one ribbing. Stockinet stitch is created by knitting all even rows, and purling all odd rows. If you are knitting in the round, stockinet stitch is created by all knit stitches because you never have to turn your knitting around. Knitting in the round will be discussed in chapter 4.

Stockinet stitch, knit side

Stockinet stitch, purl side

Summing Up

All knitted garments you see are created using the knit stitch and the purl stitch. The more complicated looking knitted fabrics and laces you see are created by manipulating combinations of knit and purl stitches. So, once you have mastered the basic techniques of knitting and purling, you can have no fear facing new stitch patterns. They are all using knit and purl stitches in different ways. You now know how to cast stitches onto your needles, how to knit, how to purl, and how to put them together into the basics of the art of knitting. Remember to have patience with yourself. If you feel frustrated or confused, give yourself a break. Even accomplished knitters need to read the directions several times before the proverbial light dawns and we understand what the pattern is saying. Sometimes, you just need to take a step in faith that you can do this. You can.

Chapter Three

Creating Shaping

Knitted garments require some shaping. This is accomplished in a variety of ways with a purpose specific to the garment or item. For example, sleeves require increasing from the wrist to the shoulder; some shawls are knitted by increasing at the beginning and the end of specific rows to create a triangle; some dishcloth patterns have one increasing to a triangle then decreasing to form a square. You are now going to learn the most commonly used methods of increasing and decreasing. The first three methods of increasing and decreasing are nearly invisible. The last technique changes the orientation of the stitches in the final garment to create the decorative pattern usually seen on a jumper with raglan sleeves. I have also used it to create a pattern on the crown of a hat. Again, making practice squares to discover how these techniques work is a fun and stress-free way to develop your new skills.

'Shaping is accomplished in a variety of ways with a purpose specific to the garment or item.'

Increasing

Increase: knit twice in next knit stitch

To accomplish this, slip your right-hand needle into the back side of the next stitch to be worked. Wrap your yarn around the right-hand needle anticlockwise back to front, but do not remove the knit stitch from the left needle yet.

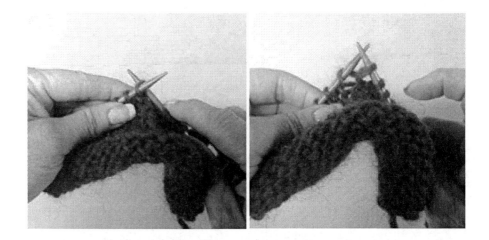

Push the right-hand needle into that same stitch on the front side from left to right, wrap your yarn as before (as in casting on).

Now discard the worked stitch. You will see you now have two stitches on your left-hand needle coming from the one worked stitch. Knit these two stitches as normal.

Increase: purl twice in next purl stitch

To do this, put your right-hand needle into the front of the next stitch to be worked from back to front, as to purl. Wrap your yarn around the right-hand needle, clockwise forming a new loop. Do not remove the worked stitch from the left-hand needle.

Insert the left-hand needle into the same stitch and remove the right-hand needle from the 'new' stitch.

Increase: knit in the stitch below

For this one, you simply insert your right-hand needle into the horizontal thread between two stitches.

Wrap your yarn around the right-hand needle pulling a new loop through the thread. Place the new loop on the left-hand needle and work it as if it were always there.

Increase: purl in the stitch below

Again, you simply insert your needle into the horizontal thread between two stitches.

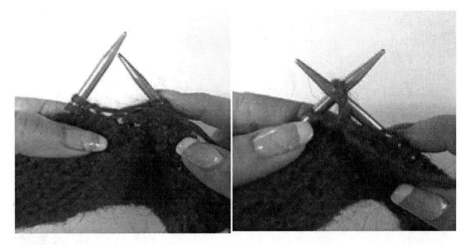

Wrap your yarn around the right-hand needle pulling a new loop through the thread. Place the new loop on the left-hand needle and work it as if it were always there.

Increase: Yarn over (or yarn forward)

This technique adds a stitch and an intentional hole. This stitch is usually paired with a decrease to create lace and stitches like willow and travelling leaf. You merely wrap the yarn around the right-hand needle, from back to front, anticlockwise, in-between two stitches. Then continue to knit.

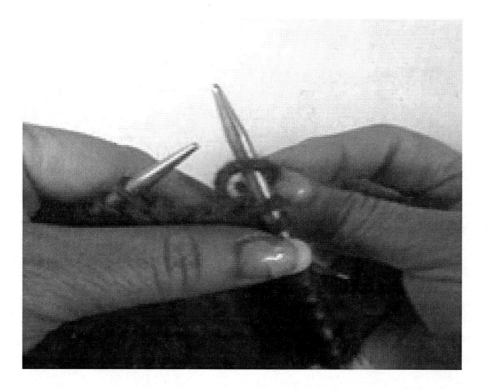

Decreasing

Decrease: knit two stitches together

Insert your right-hand needle into two stitches and knit them together.

Decrease: purl two stitches together

This is the same method, only this time you are purling.

Decrease: slip one, knit one, pass slipped stich over (sl1, k1, psso)

Slip the next stitch from the left-hand needle to the right-hand needle without working it. Knit the next stitch on the left-hand needle and discard the worked stitch as usual. Now lift the slipped stitch over the one you just knit and discard the slipped stitch, as in casting off.

Decrease: slip one, purl one, pass slipped stich over (sl1, p1, psso)

This is accomplished in the same way as the above technique, however, this time you are purling.

Summing Up

You have now learned the most commonly used methods of increasing and decreasing. The first three methods of increasing and decreasing are nearly invisible. The last technique changes the orientation of the stitches in the final garment to create the decorative pattern usually seen on a jumper with raglan sleeves. Making practice squares using each of these techniques is not only a good way to practise, it is also a way for you to see just how each one looks when put to use. You will use these techniques many times in making garments such as hats, mittens, and jumpers. Happy practising!

Chapter Four

Knitting in the Round

Knitting in the round is a very useful technique. It often seems daunting at first; however, when you become at ease with the technique, you can create seamless garments with ease. Knitting in the round also makes working in colour much easier in both the knitting and in reading charts and graphs. When you knit in the round, the only additional thing you need are stitch markers. These are little plastic rings used to mark the beginning of the round and in more complex patterns the beginning and end of sets of repeated stitches. When you knit in the round, it is important to have established a gauge swatch. Gauge is the way you can be assured that you will end up with a garment that is just the right size. This will be discussed in chapter 5.

Using four needles

When using four needles, you cast on to three of the needles; join the stitches together; and then proceed around and around until your piece is the required length. When I am knitting cuffs for mittens, gloves or sleeves, I often cast all my stitches onto one needle then slip the beginning stitches onto a second needle, then the ending stitches onto the third needle so that the stitches are evenly divided among the three needles.

'Knitting in the round creates seamless garments with ease.'

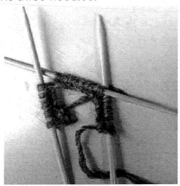

Knitting: A Beginner's Guide

41

Using the previous illustration, hold the left vertical needle in your left hand allowing the lower point of the right needle to rest under the left needle so that a triangle is formed. Now insert the free fourth needle into the first stitch on the left-hand needle and begin knitting.

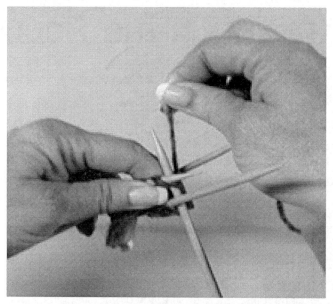

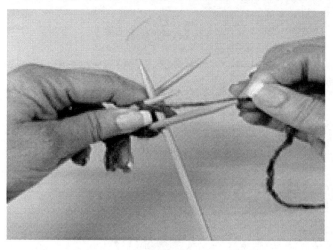

Using circular needles

Using circular needles is much less intimidating than using four needles. However, remember to mark the beginning of your round with a stitch marker. Knitting in the round is really a spiral. There is a technique illustrated on YouTube for hiding the slight hop between rounds. It is useful when one is creating an item that is heavily striped. I, personally, do not use that technique, so I am not going to illustrate it here.

When using circular needles, all you have to do when you finish casting on, is hold the end with the long end of your yarn in your right hand, and the end where you began casting on in your left. Use the right-hand point to insert into the first stitch on the left-hand needle and begin knitting.

Summing Up

Knitting in the round creates seamless garments. Using circular needles is easier at first than using four double-pointed needles; but, once you learn the technique, both types of needles are easy to use. Remember to keep your stitches straight (not twisted) and to use a stitch marker at the beginning of the round on circular needles. When you are using four needles, you can lay a short piece of contrasting colour yarn between the two stitches at the beginning and end of a round and move it up after a few rounds to remind yourself of where your round ends.

Chapter Five

Practice Patterns

The first two sections in this chapter may seem a bit tedious. However, you can avoid some of the errors typical in learning to knit if you read through them and practise them until you are comfortable old friends. Remember to have patience with yourself when you are reading a pattern for the first time. It may seem like utter gibberish; but with time and patience, you will understand and become adept at this new skill.

How to read a pattern

Reading a pattern becomes easier when you learn the short-hand abbreviations that make up the pattern directions. A full list of these abbreviations is found in the glossary, however, the most commonly used expressions are as follows:

- K followed by a number means to knit that many stitches; so K5 means to knit five stitches.

- P followed by a number, means to purl that many stitches; so P5 means to purl that many stitches.

- Increase is either abbreviated as inc. or as M1. This means to knit, or purl, twice into the next stitch.

- Decrease is abbreviated as K2tog. Meaning knit two stitches together. Also, P2tog means to purl two stitches together.

'Remember to have patience with yourself when you are reading a pattern for the first time.'

A note about tension (gauge)

Tension, also known as 'gauge', is very important when you are making a fitted garment. Tension is how you are assured that the finished garment will fit. Always knit a tension swatch in the pattern stitch you will be using. For example, if you are using stockinet stitch for a hat and the tension is 18 rows and 13 stitches to five inches, if your tension swatch has 12 stitches, then the finished garment will be one and three-quarter inches larger. In this case, use one size smaller needle. On the other hand, if your tension swatch has 14 stitches to five inches, then the finished garment will be one and three-quarter inches smaller than expected, so use the next size larger needles.

To knit a tension swatch cast on a minimum of twenty stitches and knit a square in the same stitch pattern you will be using for the garment. Cast off; then steam press the swatch in a damp cloth folding the cloth over and under your swatch. Pin the swatch to a piece of cardboard and use a gauge to measure and count stitches and rows. Each little 'V' is one stitch and one row.

'Always knit a tension swatch in the pattern stitch you will be using.'

This is a gauge set to count stitches in five inches.

This is a gauge set to count the number of rows in five inches.

Here, I have marked and labelled the swatch with the number of stitches and rows in five inches. As you can see, I am a little over the required 13 stitches and 18 rows per five inches. So, I needed to switch to one size smaller needle to knit the garment.

Hot pad or coaster

This is a good first project as there are no gauge requirements, and the finished project can be useful. Cast on twenty-five stitches using a medium weight yarn, such as a DK or sport weight yarn. Knit every row (garter stitch) until you have a square. Cast off. Tuck in the ends of the yarn using either a yarn needle or a crochet hook to weave the ends into the cast on and the cast off stitches.

Make another square using the same yarn and all purl stitches. This will let you see if there is a difference in your tension between your knit and your purl stitches.

Next, make a square using stockinet stitch, purl odd rows and knit even rows. Now you will have three squares that you can either use as a reference, or you can use them to protect your table from a hot pot.

Scarf

This next project is also knit with a DK or sport weight yarn. Use size four needles. Cast on twenty-five or thirty stitches (your choice of how wide you want your scarf). Knit the first three rows (garter stitch). Row four: purl the first three stitches and knit the row until the last three stitches; purl the last three stitches. Row five: knit the first three stitches; purl until the last three stitches; knit the last three stitches. Repeat rows four and five until your scarf measures at least three feet (again, your choice of how long you want your scarf). Then knit the last three rows, garter stitch. Cast off; and then weave in the ends. Using garter stitch at the beginning and end of the scarf, and using the beginning and ending stitches opposite of the row, prevents the scarf from curling.

Wash cloth

This next project helps you practise increasing and decreasing and provides a useful item at the finish. Select a cotton yarn in the colour of your choice. Size nine needles work well. Cast on five stitches.

Row 1: Purl two, knit one, purl two.

Row 2: Knit two, purl one, knit two.

Row 3: Purl two, make one (knit two into the next stitch), purl two.

Row 4: Knit two, purl two, knit two.

Row 5: Purl two, make one, make one, purl two.

Row 6: knit two, purl four, knit two.

Row 7: Purl two, make one, knit two, make one, purl two.

Row 6: knit two, purl six, knit two.

Row 7: Purl two, make one, knit five, make one, purl two.

right side   wrong side

You are basically increasing one stitch after the first two purled stitches and before the next two purled stitches, every other row. Continue increasing every other row until your piece measures six inches.

Now you begin decreasing stitches. On the right side rows, purl two, knit two together, knit the row until the last two knit stitches; knit two together, purl two. The wrong side rows continue as knit two, purl across to the last two stitches, and purl two to end the row. When you have decreased to the last five stitches, cast off.

right side   *wrong side*

Summing Up

You now have patterns for three very serviceable knits. You have also practised basic increasing and decreasing. In chapter 6, you will find patterns for a tea cosy, a hat and mittens. For the hat and mittens, you will be practising knitting in the round.

Chapter Six
Next Step Patterns

A tea cosy

With this pattern, you will use your gauge for stockinet stitch to determine how many stitches you will need to cast on. Measure around the fullest part of your teapot. If your gauge with DK yarn and size five needles is thirteen and one half stitches for five inches, divide by five to get how many stitches per inch you knit. Then multiply by how many inches your teapot is around its fullest part. So for an 18-inch teapot, I need 48.6 stitches. This is not possible, so I'll use 48 stitches. Divide this in half; because the cosy will be made in two halves. Thus, I'll cast on 24 stitches. Knit in stockinet stitch to match the height of the teapot. Make a second square (or rectangle depending upon the shape of your teapot) to match the first. Sew up the sides of the rectangles, leaving one section open on each side for your handle and spout to poke through. Weave a ribbon through the top and one through the bottom to snug your cosy around your teapot.

More complex, but free, patterns are available at www.ravelry.com.

Hat

Cast on 63 stitches, using DK yarn and size four needles. (US9)

Join into a circle and knit three inches in K2 P2 ribbing.

Change to stockinet stitch and work eight inches in stockinet stitch.

For the crown shaping: *K1, K2tog* (42 sts) This means to knit one, then knit two stitches together, and repeat this all around the round ending up with 42 stitches in the round. Knit three rounds without decreasing.

Next, *K2tog* (21sts) This means to knit two stitches together all around ending with 21 stitches at the end of the round.

Knit two more rounds without decreasing.

Finally, knit two stitches together all around ending with six stitches remaining. Cut the yarn leaving a six-inch long tail. Thread the tail through a yarn needle and pass it through the remaining six stitches. Draw them together tightly, and weave in the end of the tail.

Mittens

Using worsted weight yarn and four double pointed needles in size nine (US3) cast on 40 stitches. Join in a circle, with the skein end on your right and the short tail end in your left hand, as you begin the first round of knit two, purl two ribbing. Work in K2 P2 rib for desired length of wrist, about four inches. Change to size ten needles (US5) and knit three rounds.

Shape for the thumb:

Round 1: K1, P1, K remainder of round.

Round 2: P1, K1, P1, K remainder of round.

Round 3: P and K in the first stitch (1 st increased) K in the front and the back of the next stitch, (another st increased) P1, K remainder of round.

Round 4: P1, K3, P1, K remainder of round.

Round 5: P and K in the first stitch, K2, K twice in the next stitch, P1, K remainder of round.

Round 6: P1, K5, P1, K remainder of round.

Continue to increase in this manner (increase in the first purl stitch and in the last knit stitch before the second purl stitch every other round) until there are thirteen stitches between the two purl stitches. Work three rounds after the last increase round.

Following round: K1, take the next 13 stitches off onto a stitch holder to be worked later. Cast on three stitches and continue the rest of the round. Continue to knit around until the mitten is six inches long from the end of the ribbing.

Shape for the top of the mitten:

Round 1: *K1, K2tog, K13, slip1, K1, psso* Repeat between the *s once more.

Round 2 and all even rounds: Knit around.

Round 3: *K1, K2tog, K11, slip1, K1, psso* Repeat between the *s one more time.

Round 5: *K1, K2tog, K9, slip1, K1, psso* Repeat between the *s one more time.

Round 7: *K1, K2tog, K7, slip1, K1, psso* Repeat between the *s one more time.

Round 8: Knit around.

Bind off – fold so that the decreases are at the sides and sew the top shut.

Thumb:

Pick up the thirteen stitches from the stitch holder and the three cast on stitches dividing them among three needles, five on each of the first two needles and six stitches on the third.

Join and knit around, decreasing one stitch at the inside of the thumb on the first and second rounds. Work straight until the thumb measures ½ inch from fingertip.

Shape the top of the thumb:

Round 1: *K2tog, K3* Repeat between *s around.

Round 2: Knit around.

Round 3: *K2tog, K2* Repeat between *s around.

Row 4: K2tog around.

Cut yarn leaving a six-inch tail. Thread the tail through a yarn needle and thread it through the remaining loops. Draw the stitches tightly together and secure the end of the tail by darning it in on the wrong side of the thumb.

Make a second mitten just like the first.

Summing Up

You have learned quite a lot already. With the patterns for a hat and mittens, you can add a scarf and knit away happily for years. Remember to use a stitch marker at the beginning of a round to help you. You can also use your gauging skills to determine the number of stitches you need to cast on in order to customise a hat for someone special.

Chapter Seven
Textured Knits

This chapter will introduce you to some textured patterns using the stitches you already know. Putting the basic stitches together in interesting ways results in the textures you will see. You can practise these stitches by making squares, or incorporate them into a hat or a scarf.

Basket weave stitch

'Basket weave stitch is an easy textured knit. It looks great for a jumper too.'

Cast on a multiple of six stitches.

Row 1: Knit across

Row 2: *K3, P3*

Row 3: *P3, K3*

Row 4: *K3, P3*

Row 5: *K3, P3*

Row 6: *P3, K3*

Row 7: *K3, P3*

Repeat rows 2 to 7.

Crow's foot stitch

Cast on a multiple of four stitches and add one more.

Odd rows: Purl across.

Even rows: K1, *M1, slip1, K2, psso* Repeat between *s across the row.

Travelling leaf stitch

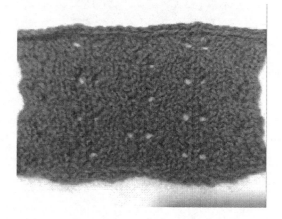

Cast on a multiple of twelve stitches then add five more.

Row 1 and every odd row: Purl across.

Rows 2 and 4: K2, *K1, yo, K3, K2tog, K1, slip1, K1, psso, K3, yo* end row with K3.

Rows 6 and 8: K2, *K1, slip1, K1, psso, K3, yo, K1, yo, K3, K2tog* end row with K3.

Repeat rows 1 to 8.

Willow stitch

'Travelling leaf stitch looks elegant for a shawl or a jumper.'

Cast on a multiple of ten stitches and add three more.

Row 1: K2, *yo, K3, slip1, K2tog, psso, yo, K1* end row with K3.

Row 2 and all even rows: Purl across.

Row 3: K2, *K1, yo, K2, slip1, k2tog, psso, K2, yo, K2* end row with K1.

Row 5: K2, *K2, yo, K1, slip1, K2tog, psso, K1, yo, K3* end row with K1

Row 7: K2, *K3, yo, slip1, K2tog, psso, yo, K4* end row with K1.

Row 8: Purl across.

Repeat rows 1 to 8.

Summing Up

Textured stitch patterns are a great way to add interest in a single colour knit. Crow's foot stitch, made with a fine yarn would make a beautiful pair of mittens. Using a heavier weight yarn, such as an Aran, would make a lovely throw, or in a chunky weight yarn, a pillow cover. I used basket weave stitch for my very first jumper and travelling leaf stitch for my second. Willow works better with a firmer yarn than the alpaca pictured here. Practise these stitches using squares at first. That way, you can decide if you like them, and how you may want to use them. I keep a little notebook next to me when I work so that I can write the row numbers down and cross them off when I finish them. You can also purchase a stitch and row counter; but I am just as happy with my notebook and pen.

Chapter Eight

Colour Works

Working with two or more colours of yarn is fun and creates beautiful items that you will love. Most patterns that you may find will limit the use of colours to two per row of knitting. Even if the overall pattern calls for as many as eight different colours, most of the time you only need to pay attention to two colours at once. You will be using both hands to hold the yarn; so, have patience with yourself as you master yet another skill.

How to hold the yarn

Just as before, hold the main colour in your right hand. Weave the second colour through the fingers of your left hand over and under as illustrated below.

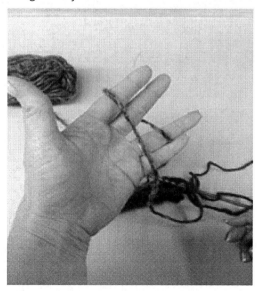

Use your index finger to hold the second colour and the right-hand needle to catch hold of the yarn.

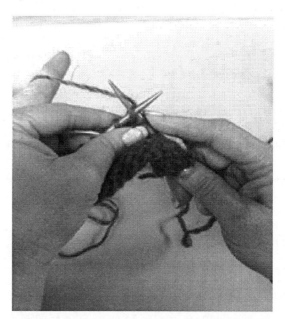

With practice, you will be able to knit fluidly with little effort. This will leave you able to pay attention to the colour pattern and to enjoy your work. Knitting in the round with colours is the easiest way to work in colours. Knitting on straight needles, requires that you purl the wrong side rows without using a second colour except in the use of stripes.

How to carry over

When a colour is not knit for five or more stitches, it needs to be carried over on the back of the work. This is most easily accomplished by slipping it between the colour being worked and the needles prior to wrapping the working colour around the needle. This carries the non-working colour across the back of your piece without it leaving a big loop.

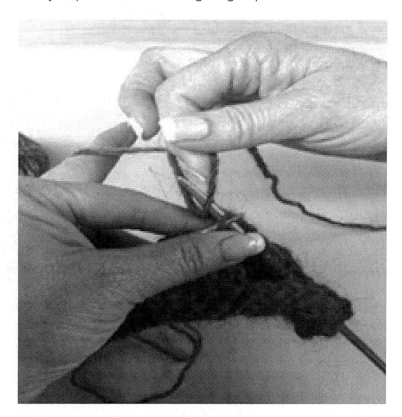

How read a colour chart

Colour charts show you where each colour should be knit. They begin at the bottom right-hand side of the chart and are read right to left, then left to right for the second row, then right to left again for the third row, and so on. Charts are easier to pick up and use if one is quite visual by nature. For someone who is more verbal by nature, one could write out the chart in words.

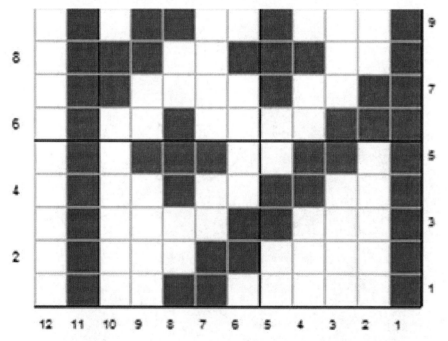

This chart is used in a pattern called Coal Spring Scarf.

This chart in words would begin with 'knit one brown, five white, two brown, two white, one brown and one white'. You would repeat these twelve stitches around the first row. Then you would begin the second row and read the stitches from left to right, repeating the same twelve stitch patterns around the row. The entire pattern may be found online at www.knittingincolor.blogspot.com The blog is dated 7 March 2010.

Summing Up

Working in colour is a great way to add pizazz to your knitting. Take your time, and practise on smaller pieces such as hats until you are very comfortable with the process. Once you have added working in colour to your knitting repertoire, you will feel confident to tackle any colour pattern with confidence. I photocopy colour charts so that I can check off rows as I knit them. This is also where additional stitch markers come in handy. You can place a stitch marker between sets of repeated pattern stitches. For example, if the colour pattern is 20 stitches wide, you can place a stitch marker after every twentieth stitch. Plus, if I have set aside a project for a length of time, it is very helpful to know just where I left off.

Chapter Nine

Your First Jumper

Knitting for family and friends is rewarding, especially when you see their joy when they receive what you have put time and love into creating. The infant jumper pattern minimises sewing up at the end. The body of the jumper is knit in one piece until the underarm; then stitches for the back and one side are slipped to a holder and reserved for later. The infant jumper is tied with ribbons sewn onto the finished jumper. The child's jumper has wide stripes to resemble a rugby jersey. The adult jumper is plain; so, you may decide to choose a textured stitch pattern, a variegated yarn colour, or a self-striping sock yarn. Remember, take your time and enjoy.

'Remember, take your time and enjoy.'

Infant jumper

Materials: 4 skeins baby yarn, size 9 needles (US 4) ribbon.

Gauge: 13 stitches for 2 inches, and 9 rows for 1 inch.

Measurements: chest 21 inches, length 11½ inches, width of sleeve 7½ inches.

Back and fronts:

Cast on 136 stitches

Row 1: (wrong side) P6, K3, *P1, K2* repeat between *s to within 7 sts of end, K1, P6.

Row 2: K6, P3, *K1, P2* repeat between *s to within 7 sts of end, P1, K6.

Row 3: Repeat row 1.

Row 4: Repeat row 2.

Row 5: Repeat row 1.

Row 6: Knit all stitches.

Row 7: P6, K1, repeat between *s of row 1 to within 6 sts of end P6.

Row 8: K6, P2, repeat between *s of row 2 to within last 8 sts and then K1, P1, K6.

Row 9: Repeat row 7.

Row 10: Repeat row 8.

Row 11: Repeat row 7.

Row 12: Knit all stitches.

Row 13: P6, K2, repeat between *s of row 1 to within last 8 sts, then P1, K1, P6.

Row 14: K6, P1, repeat between *s of row 2 to within last 6 sts then K6

Repeat rows 13, 14, and 13.

Row 18: Knit all stitches.

Repeat these 18 rows of pattern until about 7¼ inches from beginning, end with the 11th pattern row.

Next row: (right side) K31 then slip to holder for right front. Cast off 7 sts for first underarm; K60 then slip those 60 to holder for the back. Cast off 7 sts for the second underarm, K31.

Left front:

Work pattern on 31 sts until 2 inches above the underarm, end on wrong side with the 11th pattern row.

Next row: K25, slip last 6 sts to hold for yoke.

Turn, cast off 3 sts at the beginning of this row for neck edge, and then finish the row. Continue pattern, decrease 1 st at neck edge every row 11 times. Work one row without decreasing.

Next row: Cast off 6 sts from armhole edge and then finish the row. Work one row; cast off 5 sts. (11 sts for shoulder.) Do not cut yarn.

Yoke (Neckband):

Working from right side, pick up and K20 sts from neck edge; slip the 6 front border sts to free needle; K these 6 sts. (26 sts) P one row; K one row; P one row;

1st decrease row: K5, *K2tog, K5, repeat from * twice (23 sts)

P one row; K one row; P one row.

2nd decrease row: *K4, K2tog, repeat from * twice, K5 (20 sts)

Cast off as to purl.

Right front:

Slip the 31 stitches from holder onto needle. Beginning at underarm, work until two inches above underarm, ending with 12th pattern row.

Next row: Work 25 sts, slip next 6 sts to holder.

Turn, cast off 3 sts at the beginning of the row. Continue working following Left Front directions. Cut off yarn after the last row of shoulder shaping.

Yoke (Neckband):

Take up and K the 6 border sts. Working from the right side, pick up and K 20 sts on neck edge to the same needle. Finish as for left front yoke.

Sleeves:

Cast on 36 stitches; work K1, P1 rib for one inch.

Next row: Work ribbing and increase 1 stitch in every 6th stitch. (42 sts)

Row 1: (wrong side) K1, *P1, K2, repeat from * Continue pattern increasing one stitch each side every 1½ inches 3 times. (48 sts.) Work in pattern until sleeve measures 7 inches from beginning and ending with the 11th pattern row. Cast off 3 stitches at the beginning of the next 8 rows. Cast off 24 stitches. Make a second sleeve just like the first.

Sew seams with yarn and a yarn needle. Sew in sleeves with sleeve seam at centre of underarm, and fullness gathered in at top. Sew on ribbons with thread and a needle for fastening the front.

Child's jumper

The instructions are given for size 6 with changes for sizes 8, 10 and 12 in brackets. ( )

Materials: Sport weight wool yarn in 2 ounce skeins.

Main colour – M 8 (9, 11, 12) Contrasting colour – A 3 Contrasting colour – B 3. Two sets of needles: sizes 9 and 7; and one set of double pointed needles, or a 16in circular needle, size 9. Stitch holders.

Gauge: 5 sts and 6½ rows per one inch using size 7 needles.

Measurements	6	8	10	12
Chest	27	29	31	33
Length	16.5	17.75	19	20.25
Sleeve seam	12.5	13.5	14.5	15.5

Back:

Cast on 68 (72, 76, 80) stitches with colour A and size 9 needles. Work 8 rows in K1, P1 ribbing. (Cut yarn off after each stripe leaving a six-inch tail to weave in later.)

Cut yarn and switch to M and size 7 needles. Work in stockinet stitch for 6 rows with M, then cut yarn and work 10 rows with B, 6 rows with M, and 6 rows with A. Continue with M until piece measures 10 ½ (11 ¼, 12, 12 ¾) inches from beginning, or until desired length, ending with a purl row.

Armholes: Cast off 3 (3, 4, 4) stitches at the beginning of the next two rows, then decrease one stitch on each end on the next, and then every other row, to 52 (54, 56, 58) sts. Work 1 (3, 3, 5) rows without decreasing, ending with a purl row. Begin stripes with 6 rows of A; 6 rows with M; 10 rows with B; then continue with A until armhole measures 6 (6 ½, 7, 7 ½) inches from first shaping, ending with a purl row.

Shoulders: Cast off 7 (7,7,8) stitches at the beginning of the next two rows, then 7 (8, 8, 8) stitches at the beginning of the following two rows. Do not cut the yarn. Slip the remaining 24 (24, 26, 26) stitches to a holder.

Front:

With A and size 9 needles, cast on 68 (72, 76, 80) stitches. Work exactly as directed for the Back until the sixth row of the B stripe above the armhole has been worked.

Neck: K18 (19, 20, 21) Slip remaining stitches onto a holder. Turn. Working on these 18 (19, 20, 21) stitches, and working the stripes to match the Back, decrease one stitch at neck edge every row until 14 (15, 15, 16) stitches remain. Continue without decreasing until armhole measures the same as the Back armhole, ending at an armhole edge.

Shoulder: Cast off 7 (7, 7, 8) stitches at the beginning of the next row for the shoulder. Work one more row; then cast off the remaining stitches.

Leave the next 16 stitches on the holder for the front of the neck. With the right side facing you, join yarn at the neck edge and work to match the other side.

Sleeves:

With A and size 9 needles, cast on 32 (34, 36, 38) stitches. Work 2½ inches in K1, P1 ribbing. Cut yarn and switch to M. Change to size 7 needles and work in stockinet stitch. Increase 1 stitch at the beginning and end of the 9th row and every following 8th row. Continue increases until there are 50 (54, 58, 62) stitches on needle.

When sleeve measures 4½ (5, 5¾, 6½) inches, begin stripes. Work 6 rows with A, 6 rows with M, 10 rows with B, 6 rows with M, and 6 rows with A. Continue with M.

When there are 50 (54, 58, 62) stitches, continue without increasing until sleeve measures 12½ (13½, 14½, 15½) inches, or to desired length, ending with a purl row. Cast off 2 stitches at the beginning of the next two rows. Decrease 1 stitch at the beginning and end of the next three rows. Purl one row. Repeat these four rows until 14 (14, 16, 16) stitches remain. Cast off.

Neck:

Sew shoulder seams. With right side of work facing you, size 9 double pointed or circular needle, and using the A colour still attached to the Back, knit across the stitches at the back of the neck. Pick up and knit 18 (18, 20, 20) stitches along left side of the neck; knit across stitches from stitch holder at the front of the neck, and pick up and knit 18 (18, 20, 20) more stitches along the right side of the neck; 76 (76, 82, 82) stitches. Work K1, P1 ribbing for 10 rows. Cast off very loosely in ribbing.

Sew sleeves to shoulders, then sew up sides and sleeve seams from bottom edge to sleeve end. This will make a flexible seam for active children.

Adult jumper

Sizes: 36 (38, 40, 42)

Materials: Four 4 ounce skeins fingering weight yarn, needles sizes 13 (US 1) and 11 (US 3) 13 circular 16 in.

Measurements				
Chest	36	38	40	42
Length to underarm	15	16	16	16
Sleeve seam	19	19	20	20

Gauge: 8 sts and 10 rows per one inch.

Back:

Using size 13 needles, Cast on 130 (138, 146, 154) sts. Work in K2, P2 ribbing for 4 inches. Increase across next row at even intervals to 145 (153, 161, 167) sts. Change to size 11 needles and purl back across row. Work in stockinet stitch until back measures 15 (15½) inches, or desired length, to underarm.

Armhole: Cast off 7 (7, 8, 9) stitches at the beginning of the next two rows. Decrease one stitch at the beginning and end of every knit row until 119 (121, 123, 125) stitches remain. Work without decreasing until armhole measures 8½ (8½, 8¾, 8¾) inches from cast-off stitches.

Shoulder: Cast off 8 stitches at the beginning of each of the next 10 rows. (40 sts cast off for each shoulder.) Slip remaining stitches onto stitch holder for the back of the neck.

Front:

Work the same as the back until armhole measures 6 (6, 6¼, 6¼) inches.

Neck: With right side of work facing you, K 47 (47, 48, 47) stitches and slip them onto a holder for the left shoulder. K across centre 25 (27, 27, 31) stitches and slip onto a stitch holder for the front of the neck. On remaining 47 (47,48, 47) stitches, decrease one stitch at neck edge every K row 7 (7, 8, 7) times. Continue working until armhole measures the same as the back.

Shoulder: Cast off 8 stitches at the beginning of armhole edge every other row 5 times. Slip the stitches for the left shoulder onto needle and work to match right side.

Sleeves:

Using size 13 needles, cast on 56 (60, 64, 64) stitches. Work in K2, P2 ribbing for 3 inches. Increase across next row at even intervals to 60 (64, 68, 72) stitches. Purl across next row. Change to size 11 needles and work in stockinet stitch for one inch. Increase one stitch at beginning and end of next K row. Repeat this increase every half inch until there are 112 (116, 120, 124) stitches. Continue working without increasing until sleeve measures 19 (19½, 20, 20) from the start, or until desired length to underarm. Cast off 8 (9, 10, 10) stitches at the beginning of the next 2 rows. Decrease 1 stitch at the beginning and end of every other row until armhole measures 4¼ (4½, 5, 5) inches from cast-off stitches. Decrease 1 stitch at the beginning and end of every 4th row 3 (2, 2, 2) times. Cast off 2 stitches at the beginning of each of the next 4 rows. Cast off remaining stitches. Make a second sleeve just like the first.

Sew shoulder, underarm and sleeve seams. Sew sleeves into armholes matching underarm seams.

Neckband:

With the right side facing you, join yarn at the left shoulder. Use size 13 circular needle. Pick up and K 124 (124, 128, 132) stitches around the neck. Work in K2, P2 ribbing until the desired length. Cast off loosely in ribbing.

Chapter Ten

Troubleshooting

This final chapter is designed to help you prevent or fix mistakes in your knitting. Hopefully, you will take your time and avoid any of the hazards listed; but, if you do, here are some of the ways I have learned to handle them.

Washing your work

Treat your knitted garments like a baby. Hand wash in body temperature water with a gentle detergent and gently pushing on the garment in the water. Rinse well in body temperature water too. Lift the garment out of the rinse water and gently squeeze out excess water. Wrap in a clean, dry towel and gently squeeze some more. Lay garment out on another dry towel on a flat surface and gently reshape as necessary. Let the garment dry fully. Machine washing and drying will damage your hard work; so it is always best to hand wash.

'Treat your knitted garments like a baby.'

Tension (Gauge)

Tension, also known as gauge, is very important when you are making a fitted garment. Tension is how you are assured that the finished garment will fit. Always knit a tension swatch in the pattern stitch you will be using. If your tension swatch has too few stitches per the gauge, then try one size smaller needle. On the other hand, if your tension swatch has too many stitches per the gauge, then try the next size larger needles.

To knit a tension swatch cast on a minimum of twenty stitches and knit a square in the same stitch pattern you will be using for the garment. Cast off; then steam press the swatch in a damp cloth folding the cloth over and under your swatch. Pin the swatch to a piece of cardboard and use a gauge to measure and count stitches and rows. Each little V is one stitch and one row. Please refer to chapter 5 for a detailed description of tension.

Odd shapes

If your knitting has become wider as you progress, count to see that you have the same number of required stitches on your needle. If you have too many stitches, then you may have forgotten to discard a worked stitch. See if you can determine where you went wrong and un-knit to that point. If it is too far gone then the best method is to unravel your knitting and start again. Unravelling may not be possible because some yarns especially resist this. Do not be afraid to start over since you want to be happy with your work when you have finished. If you have the correct number of stitches, check your tension. You may be knitting more loosely as you relax and progress.

If your knitting has become narrower as you progress, then again, count your stitches. If you have dropped a stitch or two, you will see a run. Please refer to the section on dropped stitches below for how to fix dropped stitches. If you have the correct number of stitches, then again, check your tension. You may be knitting more tightly as you work. This can happen when you first pick up your knitting after a stressful day.

'Do not be afraid to start over since you want to be happy with your work when you have finished.'

Holes where none should be

If you have a hole, and more than the required number of stitches, you have wrapped the yarn over your right-hand needle twice, or wrapped the yarn over in-between stitches without working an existing stitch. Un-knit your work to just past your hole, then begin knitting again. Usually a hole will show up within the next row after creating it, so un-knitting should not be too stressful.

Dropped stitches

Dropped stitches create a visible run when you are knitting in stockinet stitch. Use a crochet hook and insert it into the front of the dropped stitch on the knit side. Hook the next strand up on the ladder that forms the run to form a new stitch. Repeat this process up to the top of the ladder and place that stitch back on the needle.

To pick up a dropped purl stitch, you need to insert the crochet hook through the back side of the dropped stitch. Raise the loop above the next strand in the ladder; hook the strand. Then, you need to remove the hook and repeat the process all the way to the top of the ladder.

Handling frustrations

The easiest way to avoid becoming frustrated as you are learning to knit is to give yourself permission to make mistakes. Mistakes are how we learn. Also, avoid putting pressure on yourself to finish a project by a specific deadline. If you are able to take your time and enjoy the process, you will be much happier throughout and more satisfied with your results. Reading the directions several times is also helpful. Yet, there are times in which you just have to take a step in faith and follow the directions.

'Mistakes happen. Most of the time, you are the only one who will know.'

Summing Up

Mistakes happen. Most of the time, you are the only one who will know that you forgot to change needle sizes, or put in two rows of colour when there should have been three. Un-knitting can be frustrating; but it is necessary when a bigger mistake will mar the look of your finished work. Sometimes the only fix is to rip it all out and start over. This is all right; all knitters have had to do it at one point or another, so you'll be in good company. Give yourself the gift of time and patience. You are learning a new skill that your body needs to practise in order for your muscles to remember and feel comfortable with the process.

Knitting clubs are a good way to learn from others and to socialise at the same time. Many local yarn shops have groups that meet either formally or informally on a particular day or evening. Knitting for charities is also a great way to contribute to a cause. You may decide to contribute hats to patients at a cancer treatment centre, or for newborn babies in hospital, or to knit squares for babies and children with AIDS in South Africa, or maybe even for dogs at a rescue home. For whomever you knit, your gift will be received with joy, even when the recipient is you yourself.

Happy knitting!

Glossary of Abbreviations

K	knit
P	purl
RS	right side
WS	wrong side
alt	alternate
beg	beginning
cont	continue
dec	decrease/decreasing
foll	following
in	inch
ins	inches
patt	pattern

psso	pass slipped stitch over
rem	remaining
...	repeat instructions between asterisks
rnd	round
rnds	rounds
sl	slip
st	stitch
sts	stitches
st st	stockinet stitch
tbl	through back of loop
tog	together
yf	yarn forward (same as yo)
yo	yarn over
M	main colour
A,B,C...	contrasting colours
XS	extra small

S   small

M   medium

L   large

Help List

Artesano

www.artesanoyarns.co.uk
This website includes an interactive map for stockists in your area. They include links to free patterns and to information about all their yarn colours.

Ball and Needle

www.ballandneedle.co.uk
This is a one-woman shop, reasonably priced, and includes easy kits.

Ball Hank & Skein

www.ballhankandskein.com
Based in the UK, this is a luxury yarn (alpaca and silk blends) and accessories shop. They offer free shipping in the UK and Europe.

Fiddlesticks

www.fiddlesticksdevon.co.uk
This shop is located in Devon. They offer six hour workshops in Honiton that work on a variety of skills and include a light luncheon and drinks. They also offer an online blog and an online newsletter.

Great British Yarns

www.greatbritishyarns.co.uk
This shop is located in Bath. They offer knitting workshops at their location for £25-35.

Knit A Square

www.knit-a-square.com
Knitting for AIDS orphans in South Africa:
Send squares to: Knit-A-Square, Private Bag X900, PO Bryanston, 202, South Africa

Please write on the package, 'Knitted squares for charity only. No commercial value'. This way the workers will not have to pay an import tax on your donation. Please refer to the website for more information.

Knittingyarns.co.uk

www.knittingyarns.co.uk
This website states that they are Honora Wool Specialists, and offer yarns from seven manufacturers including Rowan, Debbie Bliss and Twilly's of Stamford. They are a bit pricey, but high-quality yarns.

Loveknitting.com

www.loveknitting.com
This site offers a full range of knitters' needs.

Online knitting communities:

www.craftbits.com

www.dailyKnitter.com – Offers a pattern a day, free.

www.elann.com

www.freepatterns.com

www.knitpicks.com

www.knittingforcharity.org

www.knitty.com

www.p2designs.com – This is also a knitting for charity community.

www.ravelry.com

Book List

Knitting 20 Simple & Stylish Wearables for Beginners, Catherine Ham

Knitty Gritty: Knitting for the Absolute Beginner, Aneeta Pel

Leisure Arts: Teach Yourself to Knit

Leisure Arts: 10-20-30 Minutes to Learn to Knit

Sterling Publishing Knitting School (This book is not for the absolute beginner.)

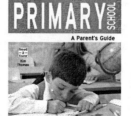

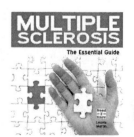